TASSONOMICA

on a botanical garden

n°1

with texts and images of
Giovanni, Marco Chiri; João Gomes da Silva;
Davide Pisu; Giaime Meloni

My initial idea was for this book series to be in one way or another "essential". My opinion was that I could have guided it and developed at least a few of the topics covered in it, only on the condition that it would be truly useful. But useful to whom? Who would really feel the urge to read these short, printed texts? Certainly I didn't, and still don't, have the ambition to contribute substantially to the theory of the project nor to elaborate on themes that are so eccentric that they raise the interest and curiosity of only a few academics in the field. On the other hand, I admit that the mere idea of writing one – or more – strictly educational texts bored me.
Returning to the basis of the discipline and using them to rebuild a way of working has, in a way, a fundamental value and – though this may seem audacious – is highly exciting.

GMC

Tassonomica. On a botanical garden
by Giovanni, Marco Chiri

With texts and images of:
Giovanni, Marco Chiri , João Gomes da Silva, Davide Pisu

Foreword by: João Gomes da Silva

....
prefazione
by João Gomes da Silva

Botanical gardens as potential spaces

Botanical Gardens are powerful tools for knowledge and experience. Since people started to domesticate plants, a specific place was needed for their selection, crossing and hybridization. This place had to be separated from other ones. They had to be protected and offer appropriate shelter for selected plants as 'natural artifices'. What differentiates one garden where selected plants are collected and organized according to their characteristics or origins from another where plants are organized to benefit from the best spatial and microclimatic conditions to grow is their purpose. One is created as a 'natural artifice' to offer a collection of plants from exogenous places in their biodiversity; this is called a Botanical Garden. The other is organized and prepared in such a way as to cultivate selected plants in the best conditions, to produce certain parts of the plants like fruits, roots or leafs in quality and quantity; this is called a productive garden, like the orchard or *Hortus*. One offers the experience of biodiversity and knowledge, while the other gives us the benefit of creating quantities of plants that are useful for nutrition or the production of fibres. We may then think that both kinds of garden are ways of perpetuating plants in their variety and genetic complexity, spreading them to places distant from their origins; substituting their natural capacity for dissemination according to natural conditions through different regions of the planet through the artificial process of propagation of an 'original plant' from an 'original place' into 'artificial habitats' recreated to allow this cultural process of plant reproduction no matter what our objectives of collection or production are.

Botanical Gardens were the expressions of the evolution of scientific thought, in which, at first, 'evidence' of the context (the region ecosystem) was stated in a methodical way through the organization of collected plants, followed by the experimentation of their reproduction (through seminal or vegetative reproduction). Then came the need to collect plants as an attempt to gain knowledge and experience of the 'strangeness' of exotic plants. They became places for knowledge and experience, as well as for strategic reproduction of plants for new food and fibre production. Today, we recreate ecosystems in gardens (or we preserve them '*in situ*' as natural reserves) in an attempt to maintain our biodiversity, as a strategy for the preservation of the genetic variety of food and fibre plant production, but also for cultural and philosophical reasons to preserve nature as part of our Identity.

This raises a bioethical question about the action of transporting plants from one region into another, transforming the natural order into cultural space. We might think that the human diet (understood as the ecological expression of the relation between people and the environment) is so detached from ecosystems today that we can no longer imagine that what we eat is the expression of a regional ecosystem. Can we imagine the typical contemporary Mediterranean diet without considering the tomato (originating in South America), the orange (coming from East Asia), the grape or wheat (both from the middle East)? But in another sense, this redistribution of plants throughout the different regions of the world and their accumulation in Botanical Gardens or their propagation in agricultural spaces is sometimes a way of preserving genetic biodiversity because sometimes these plants no longer exist in their original places in their natural form and environments.

This ambiguity is one of many paradoxes of the Anthropocene era which we no longer can evaluate things as 'good' or 'bad' or as 'right' or 'wrong'. This is also a bioethical question to be raised and considered in our contemporary vision of Space, Time and Place. If Botanical Gardens were at first places of redistribution, accumulation and acclimatization of foreign plants, in which the role of strategic collection was political, scientific, economic, or aesthetic, what is the role of those places in today's reality when we see those plants in our public gardens, streets or fields? We should consider that, as it was conceived, the Botanical Garden still preserves its role and importance, not only as a testimony and experience of the (no longer) exotic, but also as a testimony or document of different cultural positions expressed in time through the form of Botanical Garden. What, then, is the contemporary form of the Botanical Garden and its role, accepting that we should preserve the preceding form and typology of this kind of garden?

JGDS

Index

5
....
foreword

12
....
form and archetypes of the botanical garden

30
....
taxonomy embodied: a brief history of classification spaces

46
....
mise en forme

70
....
ordinary and unnatural

78
....
the Gardens at *Mar da Palha*

86
....
reasoned bibliography

88
....
credits

90
....
carnet

"Now the Lord God had planted a garden in the east, in Eden.."

Genesis 2, 8-14

CHAPTER ONE

chapter ONE

form and archetypes of the botanical garden

A "*botanical garden*" is an artificial environment created to produce, collect and classify a wide variety of plants for scientific, medical or educational purposes. Its recreational use is indeed a parallel consequence that distinguishes a botanical garden from a '*garden*' or a '*park*', with which it is often confused. Such clarification would not be necessary if it were not for the fact that today, more than in the past, with the decline of their original functions, botanical gardens often tend to encompass the recreational dimension. Currently, botanical gardens open to unorthodox practices. They are organised around the necessity to associate traditional taxonomy with formal and aesthetic criteria, typical of pleasure gardens. In this latter case, the use of the term Botanical Park might seem appropriate. This thinking refers primarily to the relationship between the form of the botanical garden and its function, a relationship that cannot be underestimated without the risk of losing its very reason for existence.

*

The tradition of the botanical garden undoubtedly finds its root in the medieval *horti sanitatis*, a particular variation on the Roman *hortus conclusus*, which, until the 16th century, was usually located near monasteries, abbeys and the schools of pharmacy and medicine at European universities.

Among the many well-known religious precepts, the Benedictine Rule (of the order of Saint Benedict), promulgated by Saint Benedict of Norcia in 534 AD, was imposed on the order throughout Europe. The rule introduced the requirement to provide monasteries with *horti* and *pomaria*: the former referring to the cultivation of medical plants, the latter to fruit plants. Arguably, the first Western herbarium was founded in Salerno in the 14th century to support studies at the *Scuola Medica Salernitana*. Matteo Silvatico (1285-1342) was an important figure involved in two seminal events. The first was the diffusion of two tomes: *Opus Pandectarum Medicinae* (also known as *Liber cibalis et medicinalis Pandectarum)*, written in Naples in 1317, and *Ortus Sanitatis,* printed in the 16th century. In these two works, the medieval physician illustrated various herbs and their uses in medical practice. The second event was the creation of the *Giardino della Minerva*, a garden of simples that can be considered one of the precursors to the modern botanical garden. Physicians harvested plants from the garden to extract their active principles (the simple, from the Latin *medicina simplex*) for therapeutic purposes and teach students about their properties and names (*ostensio simplicium*). The *Scuola Medica Salernitana* was based on Greek and Latin traditions with Arab and Hebrew influences. Their theoretical

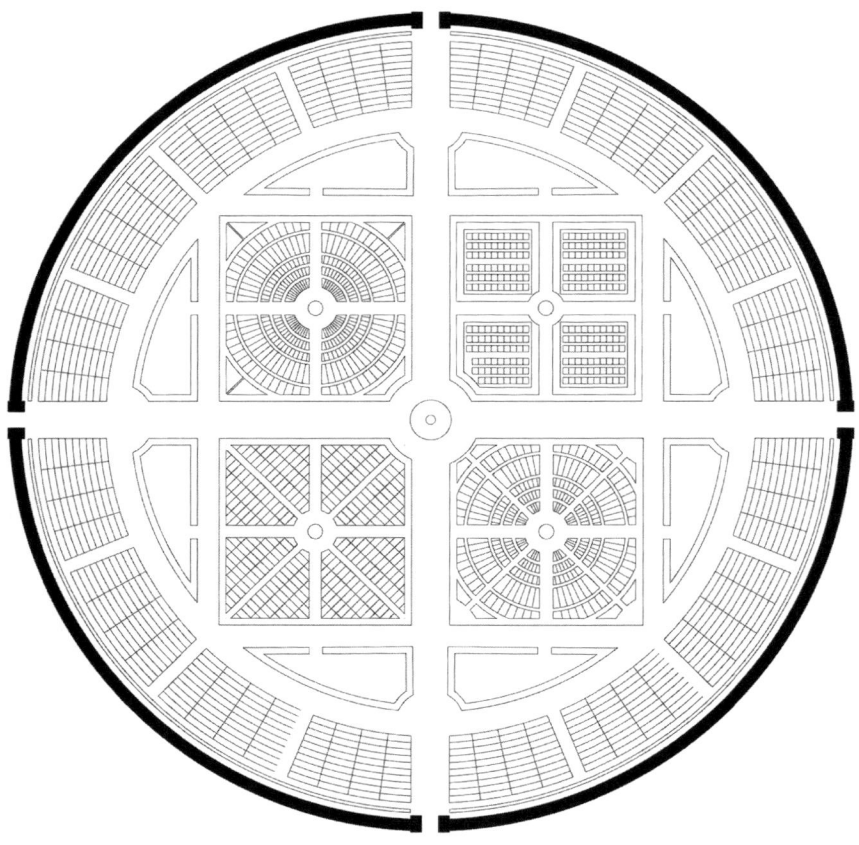

Botanical garden of Padova

bases refer to the principle of "four moods" described by Hippocrates and Galen, which spread throughout the Mediterranean in the works of the Muslim scholars Avicenna and Rhazes.

The "garden of simples" therefore developed in parallel to the 'pleasure garden', often with similar typological and formal features.

The common root of the Roman *hortus conclusus* ensured that both spaces were closed to the exterior, commonly surrounded by walls or sometimes a cloister. In a sense, they were independent spaces whose function (contemplative or scientific) was contained within their boundaries. Their form was generally square (or quadrangular) and divided into four parts by a cross with a well or a spring at its centre. This form (which is common in Arab and Persian gardens) was understood by many to be a diagram of a cosmological paradigm and thus, an earthly representation of paradise. The four-part Islamic garden was clearly a representation of the biblical "Garden of Eden". The word Eden has Sumerian origins and means 'steppe' or 'plain' or, by extension, 'arid desert', while paradise in Hebrew is referred to by the expression *"Gan'Eden"* meaning 'garden in the desert' namely an oasis.

Genesis 2, 8-14

[8] And the Lord God planted a garden eastward in Eden; and there he put the man whom he had formed.

[9] And out of the ground made the Lord God to grow every tree that is pleasant to the sight, and good for food; the tree of life also in the midst of the garden, and the tree of knowledge of good and evil.

[10] And a river went out of Eden to water the garden; and from thence it was parted, and became into four heads.

[11] The name of the first is Pison: that is it which compasseth the whole land of Havilah, where there is gold;

[12] And the gold of that land is good: there is bdellium and the onyx stone.

[13] And the name of the second river is Gihon: the same is it that compasseth the whole land of Ethiopia.

[14] And the name of the third river is Hiddekel: that is it which goeth toward the east of Assyria. And the fourth river is Euphrates.

In the book of Genesis the oasis is life given by God; it is rich in water and trees of all kinds and offers the righteous relief from danger (and temptation).

Four rivers flow out of the oasis in opposite directions to fertilize the desert.

In the Judeo-Christian tradition, the desert is always associated with sin and evil: *"When an impure spirit comes out of a person, it goes through arid places seeking rest and does not find it."* (Mt 12:43; cfr. Lc 11:24; cfr. Is 13:21;34:14; Ap 18:2). After his baptism, Yeshua himself was *"led by the Spirit into the wilderness to be tempted by the devil."* (Mt 4:1)

The garden can thus be considered a metaphor for a spiritual shelter, a place in which the faithful can retreat safely and contemplate the gifts of creation (water and fruits of the earth). In a certain sense, it is the allegory of life itself given by God to humans.

When, during the Renaissance, pleasure gardens (and gardens, as a consequence) began to open to the outside world " [...] *in a way that the eye, without constrictions of walls or emblems, can freely wander on the sight of pleasant landscapes*" (L.B. Alberti, De re aedificatoria, IX, 2), they did not lose their basic formal features but instead maintained their overall square (or quadrangular) form and quadripartite division. This form and division coincided precisely with the neo-platonic principles upon which European humanistic culture was based and, in the case of *horti simplicium*, supported the need for order in the physical organization of the botanical collections.

Memorising the names and features of the plants, along with their corresponding medical usage, was necessary for anyone seeking to learn how to remedy disease. The large number of botanical species and their therapeutic properties made memorisation difficult for the scholars at the numerous emerging schools.

The mnemonic techniques first described in the ancient rhetoric treatises (the "De Oratore and Rhetorica ad Herennium" by Cicero, for instance) were then developed during the middle ages and then by Renaissance humanists (among whom Thomas Aquinas, Pico della Mirandola, Giordano Bruno and Matteo Ricci). They were based on the association between the elements to be remembered (name, shape, features) and physical places (real or imagined) as *imagines agentes*.

This technique was called "*dei loci*" (literally "of the places") and provided the opportunity to memorise plants, however complex, by means of their physical position in a given space. The ordered form of such a space was thus important for archiving botanical data and for its transmission for educational purposes.

"Botanical gardens" were born within this system. They developed and grew in quantity and importance during the 16th and 17th centuries at the main European universities. The taxonomic organisation of plant species for therapeutic purposes already existed in some form at the turn of the 15th and 16th centuries. It relied on widely disseminated treatises (like Jacob Meydenbach's *Hortus Sanitatis*, published in Mainz in 1485 and two earlier herbals by Peter Schoeffer). Their architectural typology largely derived from the Renaissance pleasure garden, with adjustments to their vegetation design in order to catalogue and communicate knowledge of plant varieties and uses in medical applications.

*

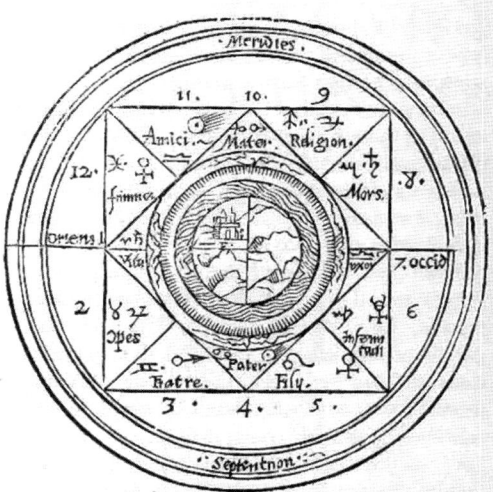

Giordano Bruno's - Ars Memoria 1582

Linneo - Systema Naturae

The configuration of botanical gardens during the middle ages and Renaissance remained essentially unaltered until the mid-18th century. Following the publication of Linnaeus' "Systema Naturae" (1758), the classification system of plant species, and consequently their organization in spatial form, underwent radical change. We owe the invention of binominal nomenclature to the Swedish botanist, Carl Nilsson Linnaeus (1707-1778). This system consists of giving two Latin names to each species: the first relating to the genre (or generic name), the second defining the species (specific name). The importance of this system of classification is that it provides a way of unequivocally attributing a name to each living organism, overcoming the subjective descriptions that characterised pre-modern herbals. The first botanical garden to implement binominal nomenclature was the Uppsala garden where Linnaeus himself worked between 1739 and 1748 (described in his book *Hortus Upsaliensis*). Subsequently King Gustav III allowed the area of the Uppsala castle formal garden, restored in the baroque style in 1744, to be used for the creation of a new Linnean garden designed by the architect Carl Hårleman. Work terminated in 1807 on the centennial celebration of the birth of the botanist. While in Sweden the first Linnean garden on the continent was being completed, in 1786 in Sicily, the "*Regia Accademia degli Studi*" acquired a plot of land near the plain of Sant'Erasmo. The French architect Leòn Dufourny (1754 – 1818), a Jacobite and Mason, designed the entrance to the new *Schola Regia Botanice* based on Palladian principles. The central building, the Gymnasium (once the location of the school, the herbarium and the library), is symmetrically flanked by two other buildings, the "*calidarium*" and the "*tepidarium*", housing tropical and temperate species respectively.

The most significant element in the complex is the "Linnean garden" placed on axis with the entrance. It was divided into four symmetrical quadrants, the quarters, further subdivided into regular rectangular beds in which the Italian botanist Father Bernardino da Ucria (author of "Plantae ad Linnaeanum opus addendae, et secundum Linnaei sistema noviter descriptae", published in 1792) located the collection of the school in rigorous Linnean taxonomic order. It is important to note that, beginning in 1500 and for the subsequent 300 years, the subject of gardens in general, and in particular 'Villa' gardens, evolved from a paradigm based on a central plan (deriving from the Roman *hortus conclusus*) to a directional plan based on a longitudinal scheme. The first manifestations can be considered sequences of architectural forms (parterre, stairs, ramps, fountains, and the palace) reaching an overall length of approximately 300m, to become, in the Baroque era, a long, autonomous promenade with immense geographic force and scale. Ostensibly, the typological evolution of the 'villa' or 'palace' garden (for instance, in the French tradition that began with the castle of Vaux and its park, designed by gardener André Le Nôtre) also influenced the overall design of botanical gardens. Consequently, they began to break down the formal boundaries of the central plan to adopt more hybrid configurations. Enlightenment botanical gardens (Madrid 1755, Lisbon–Ajuda 1768, Paris–Jardin des Plantes 1795, Palermo 1786, etc.) were characterised by their orientation along a longitudinal axis, whose extreme points were generally marked by the entrance and the main building (or buildings). Located at the midpoint, the botany school was usually composed of a regular grid of garden beds, organised into quarters and separated by the main promenades. This strategy afforded the possibility for the growth of the collections and offered the best spatial layout for Linnean taxonomic organisation.

*

When providing a systematic form for the 'character' of architecture in *Encyclopédie métodique* (1788), Antoine Chrysostome Quatremère de Quincy did not omit the definition of the character of the garden. Instead, he referred to the suitability (*convenance*) of a composition in relation to site and intended purpose. Quatremère insisted upon the expressive features of place (poetic, pastoral, exotic etc.). In doing so, he reaffirmed the categories identified by treatise writers of the time such as Thomas Whately (*Observations on Modern Gardening*, 1770, and *Essai sur les jardines*, 1774) and Jean-Marie Morel (*Théorie des jardins* del 1776). At the same time, he introduced a new series of definitions that corresponded to the particular function of the project: royal, rural, public, and academic gardens, as well as those intended for spa cities and hospitals. If on a first, basic level of the design process the 'analogical imitation' of the forms of nature (the Greek *mimesis*) endured, on a second level, another more pragmatic and rational factor came into play.

At the turn of the 19th century, the garden aesthetic became a reproduction, or better yet an idea, of nature: 'beautiful' nature. The abbot Batteux, in 1746 in "Les Beaux-Arts réduits à un même principe", recommended that artists imitate nature not as it appears in reality but as it "can be conceived by means of the spirit". The aim of the gardener should therefore consist of organising the garden in conformity with the rules of landscape beauty. Taste for the 'informal' garden codified in France between 1770 and 1800 became nonetheless widespread throughout Europe through the work of William Kent (1685–1748) and especially of Lancelot "Capability" Brown (1715–1783). Brown, as creator of more than 170 parks and gardens for the homes of the English nobility, can easily be considered the father of Anglo-Saxon 'landscape design', later defined as "picturesque". Brown's landscapes are the antithesis of Le Nôtre's geometric order and, even if they were no less artificial in their results and in the compositional process,

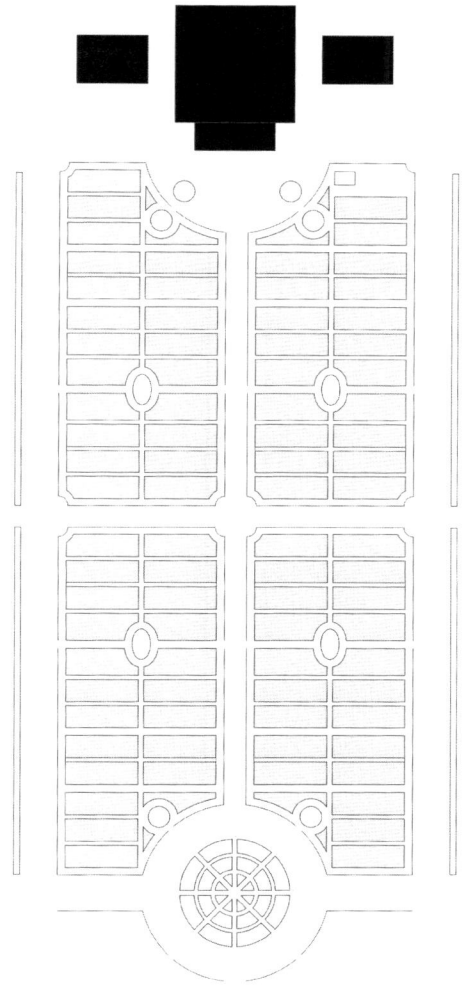

Botanical garden of Palermo. Linnean garden

nonetheless they were able to radically condition European taste.

The second question posed by Quatremere regarding the specific use of the garden, emerged forcefully during the first half of the 18th century when in England, the question of the creation of a complex system of public parks, gardens, boulevards, and squares was raised in order to provide ventilation for Britain's capital city to ease the grip of industrial smog. John Caludius Loudon's plan "Places for the Metropolis" (1829) provided for a green belt system formed by a variety of tree-lined zones with different features, characteristics and functions: botanical gardens, promenades, graveyards, playgrounds, gardens, and parks annexed to a wide range of buildings and institutions. This complex system of heterogeneous green spaces became the subject of a debate between supporters of Brown's "landscapism" and advocates of a shift towards a functionalist approach. This debate involved one of the most learned gardeners of the time, and Brown's disciple, Humphry Repton who introduced a mix between formal (useful) and informal (beautiful) areas in his later works. The publication of "Plans raisonnés de toutes les espècies de jardins" by Gabriel Thouin in 1820 provided a definitive, function-based typological organization, in which practical value coincided with a regular design, leaving the informal to pleasure gardens. Loudon coined the term "gardenesque" to describe a pedagogical approach to garden composition. In short, the method consisted of including a scientific and educational dimension in the landscapist aesthetic paradigm in vogue at the time, especiallyregarding exotic species. Thus, the distinction between the parts based on the need for plant acclimatisation became even more clear-cut in park organisation, even if this required considerable investment and qualified staff. Such an operation offered reformers the extraordinary opportunity to reveal the marvels of nature. The compositional technique of *"belting, clumping and dotting"* used to design the aristocratic gardens began to be deployed in public gardens as well as in botanical gardens open to the public. Starting in the 1850s, the common scheme consisted of wide clearings surrounded by woods with curvilinear pathways and dotted with majestic arboreal specimens thus integrating the enjoyment of natural beauty with the practical value resulting from the discovery of plant species. In this light, the pragmatic approach found in the Linnean botanical garden was tempered by a more informal and organic design. In this way, the theme of parks and pleasure gardens provided the formal paradigms for the design of botanical gardens in the western world between the 17th and 20th centuries, essentially unaltered until today.

On the other hand, their social and functional roles underwent progressive evolution. Born as places for the cultivation of medicinal plants, they gradually became gardens for the acclimatisation of plants imported from

> "Nomina si nescis,
> perit et cognitio
> rerum"

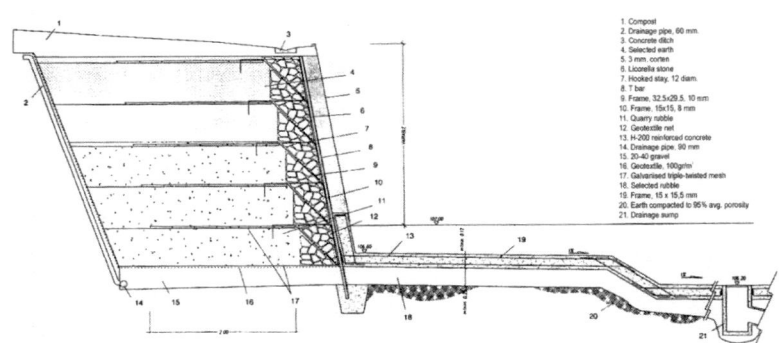

Botanical garden of Barcellona. Carlos Ferrater

abroad. In fact, they became more similar to museums and research institutions for the systematic study of natural species. Today, this function is no longer the prevalent one, as it is entrusted to or fulfilled by laboratories and specialized nurseries, so botanical gardens began to be used for education and mass communication.

In 2000, Botanic Gardens Conservation International published the "Action Plan for Botanic Gardens in the European Union", which defines the many roles that botanic gardens can play in the contemporary world. Among them: "*Seek recognition of the heritage value of BGs, raise awareness of the roles of BGs in European history, development of botany, hort. etc., promote the importance of architectural heritage in European BGs, promote an appreciation of landscape and garden styles in BGs, promote BGs as important tourist attractions.*" It is evident that, even with the prevalence of scientific dissemination, botanical gardens are also touristic, cultural and even merely recreational attractions (especially in the case of historically or artistically important botanic gardens). In this light, the divergence between the botanical garden and the pleasure garden (which historically characterised the relationship) tends to be less visible, so that formal and aesthetic considerations (in collection organisation, placement and arrangement) become more important than in the past. This requires a more complex approach that can reconcile the botanist's need for order with aesthetic and spatial quality. The botanical garden is thus positioned on a middle ground between botany and architecture, nature and artifice, scientific dissemination and recreation and leisure.

The Botanic Garden in Barcelona clarifies the role that such formal devices play today; it was designed by Carlos Ferrater, Beth Figueras and Joseph Canosa between 1999 and 2002. It extends over 15 hectares on the northern side of the Montjuic hill. The natural *cavea*, oriented towards the Llobregat valley with an optimal southwest exposure, offers optimal microclimatic conditions for the health of the vegetation. The collections are grouped according to geographic criteria while respecting ecological affinities. However, what distinguished the garden from recent botanical gardens is the fact that the architectural quality is comparable to the quality of the botanical collection. The overall design and the detail choices do not play merely ancillary roles but are protagonists on a par with the collected species and their organisation. The interpretation of the topography as an expressive design device is the key to the creation of a new landscape in which nature and artifice grow together in harmony. As much as the project is the result of a collective effort of experts in different disciplines (biologists, botanists and landscape designers), the formal invention of Carlos Ferrater and the insight that created the synthesis between the demands of the different disciplines provides its unique character.

"When we started the project for the botanical garden on Montjuic´s mountainside in Barcelona, our team of biologists, botanists, landscape specialists and architects approached it from two fundamental considerations. The first one would be to achieve a project argument which would enable the place itself to generate the scope of the intervention, revealing the form of the new landscape from its morphological and topographical conditions. With difference to other urban and architectural interventions carried out on Montjuic, to which it is completely alien, and which have the geometric layouts of universal exhibitions, Olympic games and other singular events, as their base. The second consideration would be related to the structure of the new gardens which would have to include the Mediterranean flora as well as that of other homoclimatic zones: California and a part of Japan, in the northern hemisphere; part of Chile, South Africa and a small region of the Australian coast, in the symmetrical parallel of the southern hemisphere. The geometric layout of the new gardens would base itself on botanical and ecosystem issues, as well as on the use of the concept of morphological convergence in vegetation, making it a tool of great scientific value and becoming part of the botanical gardens of next century. The synthesis of these two goals would only be possible if we achieved an instrument capable of allowing dialog and shared work between the different specialists, something impossible during the first working days. This prompted the idea of superimposing a triangular grid over the site. This grid would adapt itself to the terrain,"unweaving" itself at the edges and growing or diminishing in area in accordance with the slope. The orientation of the triangular grid would follow the three principal directions of the contours, ensuring that two ends of each triangle would always be at the same level, with zero slope." (OAB Website)

The triangular grid renders the topography completely abstract and at the same time produces a variety of concave and convex spaces that make the views and the landscape particularly enjoyable. The expressive tension of the Corten plates used to contain the discoveries and define the excavations give the ensemble a simple and reassuring beauty.

GMC

Botanical garden of Barcellona. Carlos Ferrater

"Stat rosa pristina nomine, nomina nuda tenemus"

Umberto Eco

CHAPTER TWO

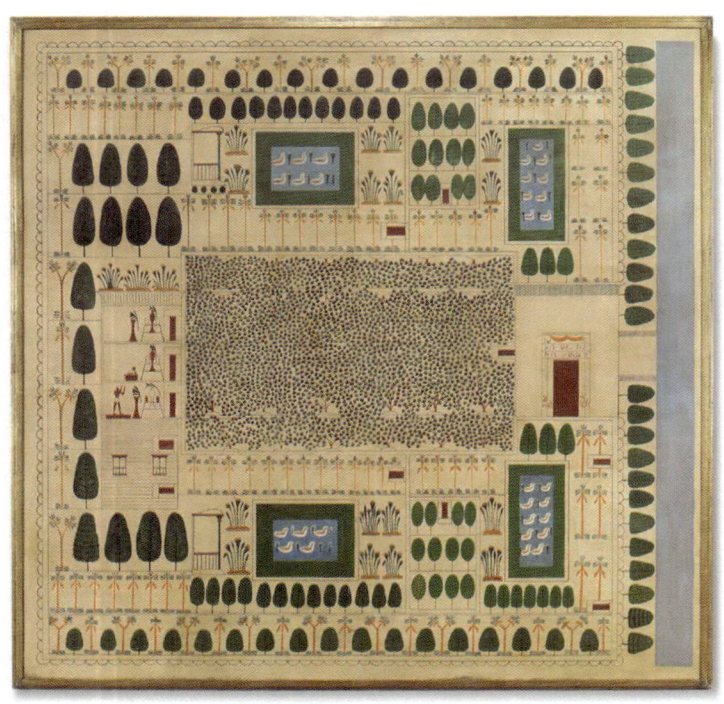

(1) *Gardens of Amun in the Temple at Karnak* in the above-ground chapel of the tomb of Sennefer Thebes West, grave no. 96 ca. 1400 BC. Drawing by Ippolito Rosellini, 1834

chapter TWO

taxonomy embodied:
a brief history of classification spaces

In its commonplace meaning, the Herbarium is a collection of dried and labelled plants assembled for purposes of knowledge and classification. Its historic origins are set in late Renaissance Italy when physician and scholar Luca Ghini began to establish the first known "hortus siccus" (dried garden) as a systematic collection of known species. This brief essay provides an insight into the origins of the Herbarium and the road to the emancipation of taxonomy from spatial constraints, relating it to places of classification, storage and access to knowledge: the library, the archive and the museum.

*

The effort to represent plants and gardens with recognizable species for knowledge and information dates to ancient Egypt with the charming depiction of a garden known as *Sennufer's Garden* (1). Only reproductions survive of this painting found in Pharaoh Amenhotep's tomb in Thebes. It communicates the desire for a naturalistic depiction of different plant species, as well architectural sensitivity, showing a spatial organization that is similar to temples like Karnak or Edfu composed of alignments of columns (or trees), symmetrical, regular courts and the central hypostyle hall, which is likely a trellised arbour in the garden (Wilkinson, 1994:6).

This correspondence between what is probably the first known garden project (Sennufer was, among other things, responsible for the gardens of Amun) and contemporary architecture tells us something of extreme importance: initially the cultivation and knowledge of plant species were strictly linked to the spatial dimension.

While in ancient Egypt interest in plants materialised around the very idea of the garden as a collection of species organized within architectural space, it is certain that in ancient Mesopotamia gardens had fundamental ties to acknowledged power. Sargon the great, founder of the Akkadian dynasty, was the son of a gardener. This suggests the importance of the knowledge of plant species at that time. It was also common to take herbs, spices and trees as plunder during military campaigns in order to grow and acclimatise them in royal gardens (Spencer and Cross, 2017).

With Theophrastus and his garden in *Lyceum* in Athens, however, a fundamental shift occurred in the study of plants. Gardens in Athens already existed but with Theophrastus, the attention of *ante litteram* botanists moved from the usefulness or enjoyment of plants to the plants themselves and their relation with one another.

Until then, people established gardens for two reasons: the enjoyment of a controlled natural environment, which we can call *aesthetic* impulse, and the creation of a repository of useful plants, a *utilitarian* impulse. With Theophrastus a third reason emerged: the discovery of nature through observation, the *scientific* impulse. The garden became an archive, a device for the study of living beings.

*

The Herbal depicts species and descriptions of their uses. Herbals have existed since ancient times, and even Egyptian scrolls like the *Ebers Papyrus* can be considered herbals, in which thirty herbal remedies and spices still in common use today are described. The most notable herbal is considered Dioscorides' "De materia medica" copied in several editions. The oldest known herbal, the *Codex Aniciae Julianae,* dates to the 6th century. It is important to highlight that the practice of copying texts for diffusion and preservation during the Middle Ages by amanuensis monks tended to distort the images. Thus, like many other manuscripts, such books needed to rely as much as possible on the power of *ekfrasis*, namely the translation of forms and colours into words, which are not prone to such distortion. Unfortunately the inaccuracy of the images, combined with the custom of medieval copyists to frequently interpret and modify books, often resulted in their not being very useful (or used), and the majority of the information about plants was likely transmitted orally or in practice. The main centres of this expertise were likely monasteries, their gardens playing a central role especially in the medical applications of plants. The diagrams of the St. Gall abbey (2) describe three types of garden: the cloister, in which we can recognise the idea of the 'philosophical garden' as Epicurus intended it; the cemetery, housing fruit trees; and vegetable and herb gardens. In the latter, the dominant geometric principle was that of a regular succession of rectangles. This garden typology is known as *'hortus simplicium'* (garden of simples) in relation to the *"medicina simplex"*, namely medications obtained from single herbs. The garden form suggests the need for an ordered collection of species, but interest in the ordering principle itself sparked later. The garden is an ordered collection of useful species in the same way the library is an ordered collection of useful information.

An important shift came with the age of printing when herbals became some of the most important scientific works of the time. Like architecture with Serlio's treatises spreading 'taxonomy', rules for understanding Greek and Roman architecture and its manipulation into new 'orthodox' buildings, herbals ignited curiosity for taxonomy and the creation of objective order by means of nature that could be studied and used. The printed herbal marked the end of the Middle Ages and a return to the same curiosity for plants that we saw with Theophrastus. Bearing important information, herbals became valuable in and of themselves. By depicting accurate reproductions

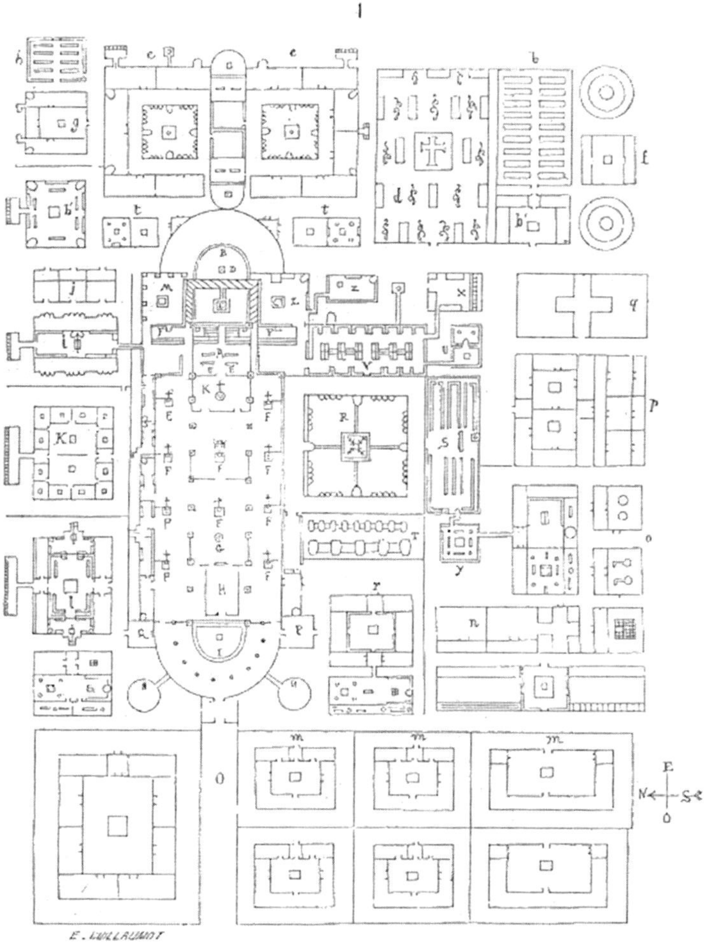

(2) The abbey of Saint Gall: on the upper left the *hortus simplicium*, on the upper right the vegetable garden, from "Dictionary of French Architecture from the 11th to 16th Century" *(1856)* by Eugène Viollet-le-Duc.

"A Ersilia, per stabilire i rapporti che reggono la vita della città, gli abitanti tendono dei fili tra gli spigoli delle case, bianchi o neri o grigi o bianco-e-neri a seconda se segnano relazioni di parentela, scambio, autorità, rappresentanza. Quando i fili sono tanti che non ci si può più passare in mezzo, gli abitanti vanno via: le case vengono smontate; restano solo i fili e i sostegni dei fili."

Italo Calvino, Le città invisibili

e   r   s   i   l   i   a

of the described species, they allowed for the creation of a shared terrain among scholars and especially among gardens, which had become true scientific institutions having the same goals as Athenian *Lyceum*'s garden.

From the perspective of scholasr interested in taxonomy, the embeddedness of the object of study within reality is only a disadvantageous burden. To lose it, while maintaining only the valuable information, would represent an undoubted benefit.

*

Let us return to Luca Ghini and his idea of pressing flowers and herbs, drying them and gluing them into books. Certainly Ghini was aware of the possibilities of print since he was born 50 years after Gutenberg's invention. Nonetheless, he invented a way not to 'represent', but to 'disembody', reality so that the studied object, in ceasing its life, became itself a quasi-two-dimensional representation of a natural fact.

The first herbaria were bound books, replicating the mainstream medium of the time. Consequently, there could have been only a limited number of specimens per book, most importantly in a fixed order.

During the 18th century and probably under the direct influence of Linnaeus' scientific activity (Müller-Wille, 2006), the custom arose of leaving the specimens deliberately unbound. Two of Linnaeus' recommendations for the establishment of a herbarium are of particular interest: (1) There should be only one specimen per sheet, and there should be only one sheet per specimen, and (2) the sheets must be left unbound. These two apparently neutral recommendations refer to the need for the specimen to represent its type, and not as a simple token. A particular specimen that acts as a referent for its species is called a "holotype".

The herbarium became something different from the sum of the specimens. In fact, beyond their simple collection, the cabinet in which they were enclosed acted as a machine for the definition of sorting criterion. Knowing it was one among many possibilities, Linnaeus chose a criterion regarding the position of the stamen and pistils of the flower, consequently dividing the species into 24 categories. A specific place in the cabinet was established for each category (3). Each shelf in the cabinet was movable according to the space required for the relative category (Müller-Wille, 2006). In any given moment, each part could be moved to another category and repositioned according to sub-categorical order. Linnaeus' cabinets represented an important attempt, as with Ramon Lull's combinatorial circle, to overcome the constraints of space in organising information.

The herbarium is an information technology device and serves as a memory support for the scholars that study taxonomy. It can be viewed as an ancestor to Vannevar Bush's Memex or another similar invention: the

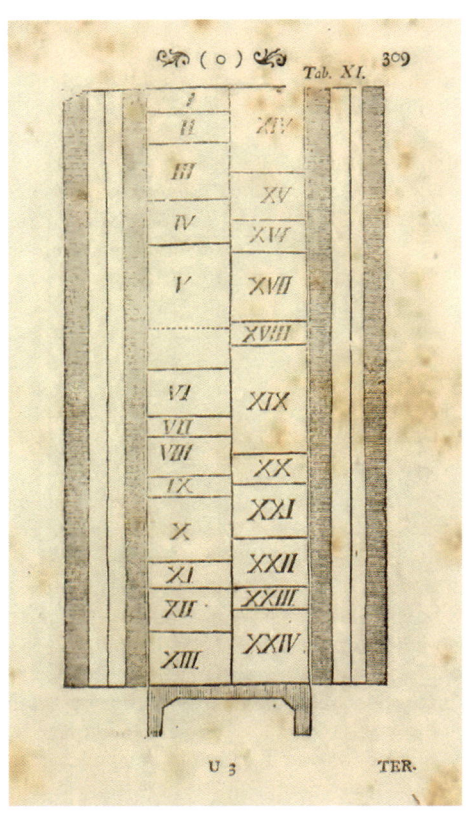

(3) Linnaeus' cabinet from
"Philosophia Botanica" *(1752)*

World Wide Web. The garden began to overcome physical constraints to take important steps toward dematerialization.

In his 1969 work, "The Herbarium: Past, Present and Future", Stanwyn Shetler called for the proper integration of computers into herbaria activities. Given the enormous number of specimens, he argued that it had become practically impossible for most curators to manage them all (the herbarium being a resource for other scholars) and at the same time conduct active scientific research. He suggested the creation of an Information Retrieval system, which would allow scholars to browse the herbarium without manipulating a single specimen. Naturally this operation would entail a loss of information but an overall process for better comprehension of nature lies at the heart of taxonomy. Today, computers have ostensibly entered herbaria, like every human activity. Index Herbariorum is a network that unites over 3000 herbaria worldwide with around 350M specimens. It contains an online collection of browseable hi-res images of dried plants with more than 3M specimens that increase monthly by about 30k specimens.

Of course, this immense collection of specimens includes a vast quantity of duplicates, but it is indeed unthinkable to manage all specimens in a single place. Furthermore every Herbarium bears its own sorting criterion based on the period of its establishment. According to Shetler there were four phases: 1. *descriptive/exploratory*, in which the aim of scholars was to find and describe as many species as possible; 2. *phytogeographic*, in which geographic distribution and endemism became the main parameters in the research on new specimens; 3. the *systematic* phase, when interest in specimens was led by the significance of taxonomy; and 4. *bio-systematic* where a single *taxa* under study led to a large collection of specimens which, until today, would have been considered duplicates.

The criteria by which Herbaria are ordered are thus a consequence of the phase in which they had initially developed. In the descriptive phase the wealth of a herbal consisted of diversity and uniqueness of the specimens; in the phytogeographic phase it switched to consistency of the supposed endemic species in a certain region; in the systematic phase the herbarium became an active instrument for the classification of species and curators used it to study possible taxonomic configurations.

As Shetler points out, it would have been unthinkable for each institution to reorganise the specimens when a new sorting criterion emerged; nonetheless, in a digitalised system it makes no sense at all to even have *one* sorting criterion, except for an indexed code that allows a specimen to be found.

The story of herbaria is far from being unique. This kind of evolution is common to a variety of fields, institutions and disciplines. Nonetheless some interesting points emerge from this story. First, while people were domesticating plants, plants were domesticating people (Spencer and Cross, 2017); a similar argument can be made for space, which people understood and learned about along with the rise of agriculture. That same space gave people the framework to devise schemes that would be of later use for the establishment of science, while setting up constraints that have proven hard to remove. An interesting account of the reflection of social structures on space can be found in Lévi-Strauss (1996): the French philosopher found that the recurrence of certain structural patterns in society can be attributed not to historical ancestry but more likely to a limited number of possible institutional combinations. As Dade-Robertson (2011) notes, an example that relates to spatial configuration is the so-called dual organization of a small society, whereby two possible village structures are the concentric and the symmetric ones. Assuming that the dual organization of a society embodied in a village can only have these two possible outcomes, we will not question which processes led to which organization, but rather which consequences are already implied in that form as emerging spatial properties.

If we take the two newly created portions of village as types through the addition of other types, we easily verify that, from a topological perspective, concentric organization allows for the creation of ever larger spaces, with the last containing the other, while a symmetrical organisation allows for the replication of single types that may not establish direct relations with the others (4). Another interesting point is Luca Ghini's invention. As opposed to other disciplines like architecture, which had the need for a medium to transform a three-dimensional object, like as a building, into a two-dimensional drawing (notably architectural plans, elevations and axonometric representations), botany, which is probably a unique case, had the opportunity to disembody its object of study and to transform it into a manageable quasi two-dimensional object. The result is something more and something less than a drawing. While the desiccation of the specimen distorts some plant features, for example colours, that a drawing would not, it does it in a somehow predictable way, and moreover, provides the possibility to study the non-evident material features of a species. Of course, printed herbals did not cease to exist, and for a wide variety of uses they represented a better instrument than the laborious herbarium. Some herbals are in fact true masterpieces. As Eco and Carriere (2017) noted, media are more likely to overlap than to substitute one another.

The final point of interest resides in Linnaeus' cabinets. These seemingly small innovations (leaving the sheets unbound and dedicating one sheet per specimen) relate herbaria both to the *Wunderkammer* phenomenon as a "mind expanding space" (Bauscher et Al., 1999) as well as to Foucault's *Heterotopias*: a series of fragments from the outside world that create, in a single place and time, a concentration that refers to different places and times, establishing a cultural link between them. Notably, interest in those very links characterises the work of the pioneers of taxonomy, and the absence of an established, physical boundary is what makes this work of classification possible. This process can also be seen in what is arguably Linnaeus' main contribution to science: binomial nomenclature, which became the logical device of taxonomy *par excellence*. In one of his most important works "Philosophia botanica", the 7th chapter, "names", begins with the famous sentence "*nomina si nescis, perit et cognitio rerum*" meaning that if you don't know the names of things, the knowledge of those things will perish. Linnaeus elaborated on his binary nomenclature theory, proposing to shrink the nomenclature in use at that time, which was a brief Latin description of the species, a method that he deemed inadequate. He suggested the use of a convention, something similar to what Shetler suggests in 1969 for the integration of IR systems into herbaria. We know that *names* relate to a *referent* through a *concept* and that names work as long as we have some kind experience of their referents. Nonetheless, we can sense the end of an era in this story. At the other end of the spectrum we can ideally recall Borges' famous list of the Chinese encyclopaedia or Eco's verse *"stat rosa pristina nomine, nomina nuda tenemus"*, which sums up the dismay of the Middle Ages represented in the arson of the library of "*The name of the rose*". Once objects have disappeared, the names do not have perceivable referents: the links have been burned.

DP

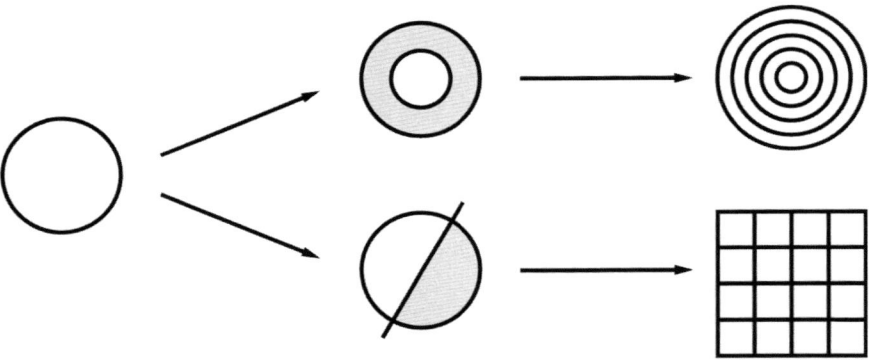

(4) The replication of types in the symmetric and concentric spatial schemes

GEOMETRY

"Se avessi ereditato dalla mia famiglia anche solo un piccolo campo, di sicuro saresti andato a fare il contadino; parlo di un contadino che coltiva solo quello che mangia, che rimarrà povero. Un bellissimo lavoro di progettazione. I contadini hanno inventato la geometria"

Enzo Mari, Intervista

Oxydendrum Arboreum, specimen scan, source: "The William C. Steere Herbarium of The New York Botanical Garden" (http://sweetgum.nybg.org/science/vh/).

Oxydendrum Arboreum, esemplare scansionato.
Da: The William C. Steere Herbarium
of The New York Botanical Garden
(http://sweetgum.nybg.org/science/vh/)

"Seek recognition of the heritage value of botanical garden"

CHAPTER THREE

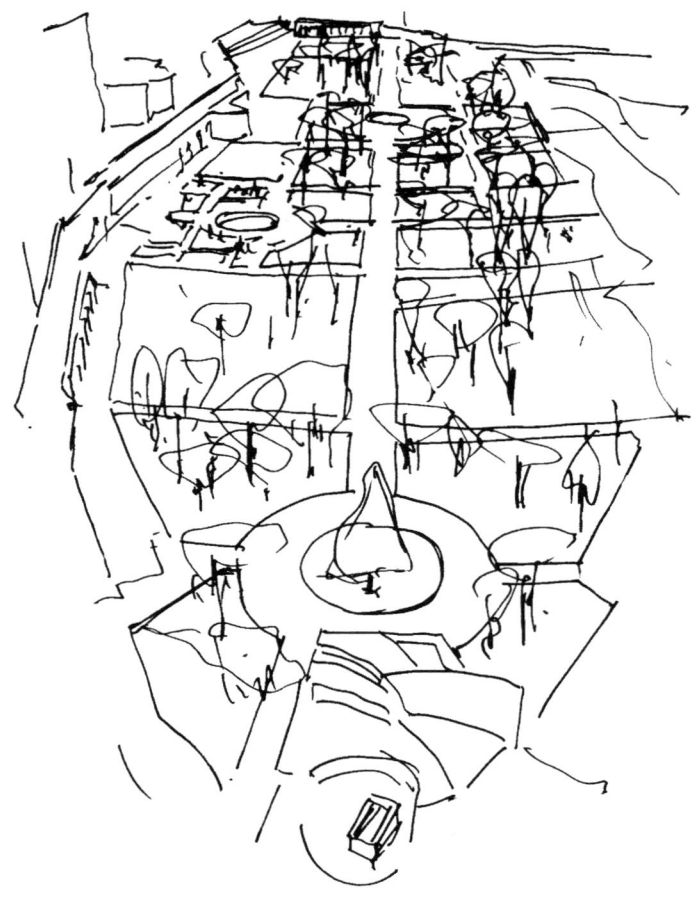

chapter THREE

mise en forme

Thus far, we have reconstructed the nexus between form and function and the social role of the botanical garden in the transition from the Middle Ages to the modern era with contemporary guidelines culminating in the document "Action Plan for Botanic Gardens in the European Union" (2000). As mentioned, at the turn of the century the transformation of the concept of the botanical garden was complete and widely accepted. Extensive analysis of this document points out the new roles of botanical gardens in terms of their cultural value on different levels above and beyond their traditional scientific functions. Aside from the conservation of plant and flower collections, in many cases the need has emerged to recover the architectural design of botanical gardens, their spatial configurations and the buildings and structures that have enriched them and modified their palimpsest over time. The need has also arisen to redefine their relationships with their urban contexts and networks of historic and naturalistic itineraries and to completely or partially transform certain parts to adapt them to new needs. It might be affirmed that the botanical garden has developed into a potential motor for urban transformation with respect to their original role that tended towards autonomy and introspection. If this is not always manifested in their physical relationships, it becomes more evident in their immaterial relationships. The botanical garden as a museum participates in a network of other similar places but even more generally, in the entire cultural infrastructure of a given context. This comes about not only due to an intrinsic value of botanical collections but also because of a garden's overall landscape quality: a setting for different kinds of events, a venue for educational activities, a support for the preservation of things of historical or archaeological value or simply a pleasant place for people. The example described in the following pages summarizes the concepts expressed thus far, offering a point of view on the topic.

*

Between 1864 and 1866 under the direction of Prof. Patrizio Gennari and with a design by neoclassical architect Gaetano Cima and master gardener Giovanni Battista Canepa, the University of Cagliari (Sardinia, Italy) created a modern botanical garden analogous to those in the major European cities albeit with some delay.

Sited among the ruins of the ancient Roman amphitheatre, another garden called the Orto dei Cappuccini and the Roman archaeological area named villa di Tigellio (on the lower slope of the hill), the botanical garden covers an area of 5 hectares. It is located at the centre of Roman Cagliari in the so-called Palabanda Valley, which is deep and long and rich with water; it was used throughout history, first for cultivating mulberries and later for grape production.

The polygonal area is approximately 300m long and measures 150m at its widest point. The geometry with its characteristic, albeit significantly modified, grid corresponds to the dictates of the botany school. The project by Canepa and Cima (who was at the same time initiating construction on his most important project, the Civic Hospital) is organised along a central longitudinal axis. The western slope is more informally designed as a result of later projects conditioned by the steep and complex topography and by the presence of Roman archaeological artefacts. Between the end of the 18th century and the beginning of WWII, at the hands of succeeding directors (among whom Professor Mameli-Calvino, mother of Italo Calvino) and head gardener Leonardo Bonsignore, who had worked very successfully at the botanical garden in Palermo, the structure grew both in quality and in terms of the wealth of the species cultivated. Post-war decline continued until the end of the 1980s when Professor Arena (supported by Roman architects Leschiutta and Roncoroni who had already worked at the Rome botanical garden) proposed a series of improvements, among which the roof over the Grotta Gennari (in reality a Roman cistern) and the promenade along the retaining walls at the southeast slope along the hospital property line. The creation of the *Hortus Botanicus Karalitanus* and the renewed enthusiasm of the director thrust the botanical garden into a more active role on the urban scene. This translates into a series of potential projects, both large and small, that can restore its role as an urban hinge connecting some of the most important places in the city.

The key feature of the Cagliari Botanical Garden, especially if compared to some of its more important European counterparts, is its intimate relationship with its archaeological substrata, which, in turn, is tied to site topography. In the Roman era, the complex hydraulic system of wells, channels and cisterns ensured a constant supply of water and at the same time provided flood protection for the city below. Destroyed by time and neglect, this system no longer fully performs this function and the soil has suffered from the effects of limited

Gaetano CIma and Giovanni Battista Canepa,
design of the Botanical Garden of Cagliari, 1861

The Roman hydraulic system between the amphitheater
and the thermal complex of the "Villa di Tigellio"

(or absent) water management, especially regarding surface runoff.

The Roman water collection system on both slopes and the *libarium* well (at the top of the foothills), which in the classical era served the arena used for gladiator contests, ensured a constant supply of water for many centuries. This conditioned the 18th century design of the botanical garden but did not compromise its formal clarity and typological coherence in relationship to other constructions.

The axial design of the botanical garden derived from European models. The botany school with its characteristic grid of closely placed planting beds punctuated by straight and slightly wider pathways was located in the level area closest to the entryway. The symmetrical circular fountains and the large main one were episodes that broke down the rigid Cartesian scheme. Where the topography interfered with the formal rule, the design first tended to adapt and then to integrate with it until disappearing. The garden composition ends at the base of the archaeological area (with the ruins of the amphitheatre as a backdrop) in a small exedra with a fountain corresponding to the location of the Roman well.

On the steeper and more irregular northwestern slope, the original checkerboard organization was substituted by a more informal design tending to establish a relationship with the ruins of the ancient Roman water system by including them in the spatial sequences of the walkways.

The Cima-Canepa project originally sought, though with some delay, to bring the scientific and formal rigor of the most advanced European experiences to the Sardinian city. However, the project was executed very gradually and with few means; therefore it could be said that it was only completed during the first half of the 20th century.

The garden, its collections and edging elements in particular were heavily damaged during WWII. Some works were carried out between 1945-1955 under the direction of professor Martinoli, in particular a stair connecting to the Botanical Institute and a masonry greenhouse. However, the plan clarity of the Cima-Canepa project had been severely compromised. The planting bed edgings (in organically formed stones embedded in the earth) were in poor condition, having lost their original alignments to the point of deforming the original arboretum organisation and rendering the correspondence between the formal idea of the Linnean beds and its spatial organization unrecognizable.

While today, as mentioned, new functions complement the original botanical garden functions, the original design is structurally conditioned by the initial concept of Linnean classification. This fact cannot be ignored when imagining a renewal project for the site. The idea of a gridded space characterized by the orderly sequence of planting beds delimited by precise edges can therefore be considered a design invariant. However, the key lies in formally interpreting this typological characteristic in order to adapt it appropriately to the changed conditions of the collections and contemporary scientific criteria.

Restoring the original spatial balance between the collection and its use and enjoyment can only be carried out through a certain degree of abstraction, since the compact Linnean grid cannot adapt to a living material that has grown over the years to colonise unsuitable spaces. This point of equilibrium was found in devising a larger grid than the nineteenth-century scheme to recover the principle of the Cima-Canepa composition, clarifying it and rendering it explicit.

If there is poor maintenance, the choice of defining the planting beds with shapeless stone embedded in the earth eventually results in them losing their form, generating a constant disruption of surface runoff. The borders become insurmountable obstacles so that the waters are forced to flow along the walkways. Furthermore, the long-standing habit of employing non-specialized workers for waste removal (dry foliage that naturally tends to settle at the base of the trees) has gradually dried out the ground so that it has become parched and impermeable.

In this condition, the water collected from the upstream catchment area (of which the amphitheatre is an integral part) is no longer intercepted by the Roman channels, and flows entirely within the garden roughly following the natural contours. Here, finding no surfaces to absorb at least part of the runoff, the water flows downstream, increasing its volume and speed along the way.

While reinforcing the formal characteristics in plan, the proposed solution reverses the relationships in section. In the project, the walkway paving constructed over the years with materials that were impermeable or rendered impermeable by compaction due to the passage of wheeled vehicles are replaced by stone blocks laid with open joints on a permeable drainage layer in order to absorb and direct storm water. The borders of the planting beds are replaced (at least in the central part of the garden, corresponding to the arboretum) by new regular elements that are 'suspended' in order to guarantee some ground-plane continuity without compromising spatial organization.

*

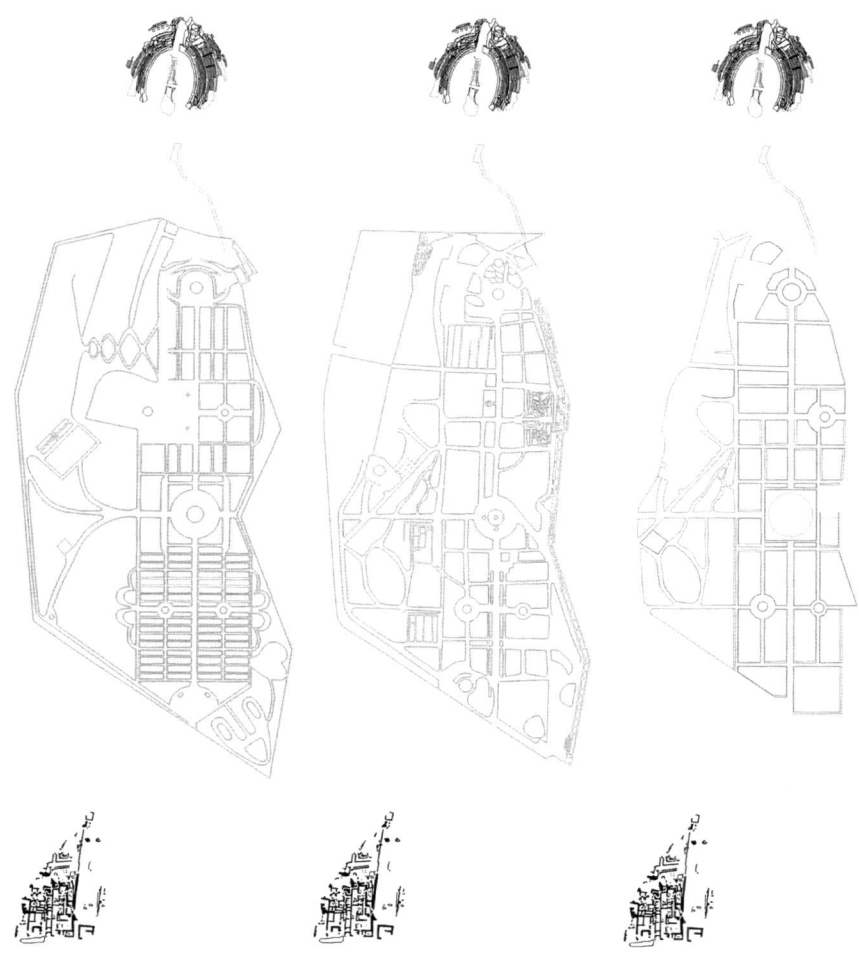

The traces of the botanical garden in the course
of time and the current proposal

Typical section of the botanical garden of Cagliari, 2017

While the classification criteria adopted by botanists are continually updated, the collections are still distributed according to taxonomic logic. Formally, this principle produces bizarre combinations sometimes lacking in intrinsic aesthetic quality. Nevertheless, the "hybrid" nature of the contemporary botanical garden - suspended between the dimensions of study and play - suggests to not overly force plant associations but to act upon the artificial component in redefining the design and its spatial characteristics. In this way, edging becomes a key element: it simultaneously defines the planting bed, supports the communication of botanical information, and becomes an element to orient and guide visits, seating, podia, pedestals and benches.

The *mise en forme* of the garden thus passes through the introduction of a new element to recover the traces of the antique, which becomes a key in the explicit interpretation of the spatial organization system supported by taxonomic classification.

As in the Botanical Garden by Carlos Ferrater, a basic geometric principle that is so simple as to be almost elementary is expressed in a variegated way, multiplying formal relationships, uses and relations among the natural substratum, the collection and architectural elements. The edging is basically a white concrete element with an average 60x60 cm section, modified to compose a vast abacus of precise solutions in relation to planting elements, thematic areas and contingent needs.

With this device, the sections of the paths that make up the garden grid on the valley floor, the surfaces of the walkways (today permeable to meteoric waters) are redefined, together with the areolas of the new grid in which the arboretum unfolds. This simple spatial organization is interrupted by some singular episodes, which, according to Cima, would have added grace and elegance to the rigid plan of the botany school. The terminal exedra (roughly corresponding to the *libarium* well) and the circular fountains, symmetrically arranged with respect to the longitudinal axis, distort the linear sequence by introducing central spaces and transversal axes. The largest one, located at about the halfway point along the main path, is the intersection of a transept that relates the large hospital volume to the east with the Botany Institute and the west slope. With this choice, the cruciform design by Cima produces a system of relationships that extends the design of the garden well beyond its natural borders involving the city in its overall composition. This formal tension is fully expressed precisely when the vegetation continuum is suspended, clarifying the relationship between the natural and the artificial.

In these places, the compact network of beds and edges is expanded, allowing the creation of more open spaces that can host the new functions required by a contemporary botanical garden. Therefore, if the relationship with the city of bourgeois modernity is mostly expressed in the cross-section, the long section reveals the dialogue with the Roman city.

The large amphitheatre cavity is located at the upper apex of the valley. Partly carved

Axonometry of the proposal, 2017

Typical section of paths and frames, 2017

into the rock (like Greek theatres) and partly - presumably- above ground supported by large, now no longer existing, arches, the arena is the most important fragment of the Roman city and the backdrop for the botanical garden spatial sequence. Although separated by a later enclosure, the artefact is an integral part of the garden, for purely formal reasons as well as structural ones. In the Roman era, the arena valley was a natural collector for rainwaters intercepted at the height of the second level balcony by a gutter that continued along carved from the rock on both sides of the valley. With this system, the water flowed downward to be stored in a sequence of underground or open cisterns. The complex hydraulic system crossing the area contributed substantially to the water supply for the Roman city located on lower ground. With the abandonment of the area in the Middle Ages, the pipes fell into disuse and the cisterns were also used as shelters. Although the Cima design does not seem to account for this underground dimension, its existence was known at the time. More recent efforts have contributed to revealing this underground network. Some cisterns, whose vaults had collapsed over time, have been transformed into greenhouses for the acclimatization of tropical plants; others can simply be visited without their true integration into the pathway system. The restoration of the hydraulic function of these artefacts is not feasible; however it might be possible to accompany them with a new network based on Roman principles, modernising them to meet the needs of today's botanical garden.

With this end, just at the limit between the amphitheatre area and the botanical garden, and on a site with no archaeological interest, an open storage tank receives the overflow from the upper basin. When this infrastructure is dry, its section redefines the threshold between the two spaces, opening them up and relating them both visually and conceptually. The lower part (open towards the garden and next to the *libarium* well) is used as an *antiquarium*.

The water is collected in a new tank system located below the on-grade circular ones and used for irrigation so the project recovers its characteristic three-dimensionality by taking root in the ground. Other small operations providing access to the underground cavities facilitate visits to these hidden places. The entrance is located at the opposite end of the longitudinal axis.

In the original design by Cima, the symmetrical composition initiates, without particular emphasis, with a small entry exedra. In fact, in the mid-nineteenth century, the area had already found its natural limit in the historic thoroughfare of Viale Fra' Ignazio. During the twentieth century, new buildings having different uses were located along this small local road between properties and its section was modified. Today, the road is narrow and cramped with no widening or sidewalk areas large enough to produce quality public space so that the entrance to the botanical garden is little more than an interruption in the enclosure continuum. The perimeter wall also prevents any visual relationship

Botanical garden of Cagliari, 2017

mise en forme

between interior and exterior, further separating the garden from the city. While the topic of the demolition of the historic wall has been debated for years, to date no agreement has been reached regarding its future. However it is still important to redefine the relationship between the botanical garden and the city, in particular its access street. This relationship cannot remain undefined for much longer.

The new role of a public garden requires greater openness to and relationship with the city. For this reason, the project introduces an access pavilion located perpendicular to the garden axis. This linear element connects the two current pedestrian and vehicular entrances with a white concrete canopy. The supporting elements are spaced so as to create a dual symmetry and offer the greatest visual permeability at the base of the building in order to create a relationship with the arboretum from the exterior. The gates, realized in hot forged iron plate with a neo-floral design by the artist Andrea Forges Davanzati, incorporate bottle-green blown glass gems that refer unmistakably to the idea of vegetation.

The example described in these pages complies fully with the strategies defined in the Action Plan for Botanic Gardens in the European Union by fully projecting the Botanical Garden into the dynamics of urban transformation and redevelopment on various scales.

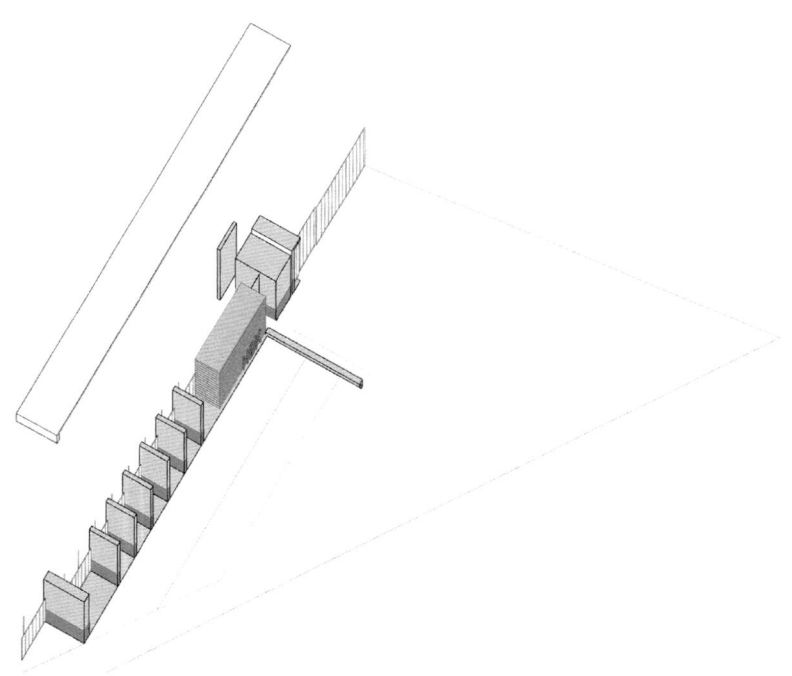

raw and abrasive

CHAPTER FOUR

chapter FOUR

ordinary and unnatural

Giaime Meloni's photographs tell a story that is quite different from what public information or an absent-minded visit can provide. The images grasp aspects that neither books nor traveller's tales can express with the same bare and brutal precision. The pleasant and romantic place that we are prompted to imagine, projecting different and alien meanings that are still appealing and exciting on the botanical garden space, is depicted here in a most raw and abrasive way.

In the Sardinian city, history determined the choice of the site for a botanical garden: a place formed by a deep calcareous valley dotted with the traces of the Roman city. Over time, that place, entirely enclosed by a wall, was surrounded by new and important buildings, some with monumental scale and character. This rather uncommon condition among botanical gardens in this category produces a continuous and constant relationship between nature (expressed in a rather simplistic way by the vegetation) and architecture that, beyond the walls or inside it, dialogue with it. But the eye of the photographer subverts the balance of this relationship. The 'nature' of the garden is represented without forcibly seeking its aesthetic value. It is narrated for what it is, without attributing any value whatsoever.

Rather, the species that are normally represented in the tidy collection of a botanical garden here appear convulsively accumulated in its exact opposite: semi-wild and real. Through abandonment and neglect, the purest form of the artificial garden is converted into its precise contrary. Meloni portrays chaotic and impure beauty where it might be easy to imagine an exact and composed field. The plants in the collection grow next to other spontaneous species with no contradiction or distress. The crowns of the trees and bushes entangle to form a living, indistinct cloud. Any attempt to return order to the plant life is in vain. Nonetheless this chaos has its own intrinsic, 'non-ordinary' beauty, here intended not in its intensity or aesthetic value but more strictly as something that is 'heterodox', extraneous to any artificial attribution of quality that is not produced by the pure accumulation of different species.

The point of view is inverted in this imprecise chaos. The plant varieties are no longer the centre of the picture nor the object of contemplation but rather simple counterpoints to what is truly important and what gave the place its origins: the city.

The disconnection that was stubbornly sought in historic parks and gardens to escape the urban dimension (perceived as the evil to avoid) is constantly annihilated by revealing the points of reference.

The search for the elsewhere beyond the walls that the author constantly grasps re-establishes the exact relationships between the walls and their urban context by inverting them. On the contrary, the decay of the architectural objects, which from time to time interrupt the continuity of the plants, likens them to the living substrate as if they cannot be distinguished from them. Storage spaces, old and new dry walls, flower beds and pots are reflected and counter-reflected in the blurry and worn mirrors of the greenhouses. The acidic eye of Meloni's photography discards the general to focus on the ordinary and banal detail.

Architecture has lost, and order has lost, the search for a precise pattern, a precise squaring, a drawer in which to store the object of contemplation that has lost significance. The complicated array of plant beds in a clumsy self-named "*giardino dei semplici*" in *beton brut* is shocked by a sprinkling of multi-coloured polypropylene vases. The neat and sharp shadow of a mullion in ductile iron hardware gives up to the shelves and containers of cuttings that adorn the interior and exterior of Martinoli greenhouse.

The balance of opposites described in the images is unstable. No one can be certain of the transformation or of the form that it will take, even tomorrow. Nature and artifice will prevail one over the other. Will they wipe each other out? Will they eventually merge? Trying to predict what will happen is not important. It is not the role of photography, which acts to fix an instant, and a precise appearance, of the flow of things. Here, an ordinary and unnatural equilibrium in 2015.

GMC

"Vos fruits aux écorces solides sont un véritable trésor; Et le jardin des Hespérides N'avait point d'autres pommes d'or"

Jean de La Fontaine

CHAPTER FIVE

Atelier © Global AP

chapter FIVE

the Gardens at *Mar da Palha*

In the early morning, light reflects onto the vast expanse of the *Mar da Palha* (the straw sea) and then it diffuses the line of Gardens along the River's Sidewalk. The atmosphere is full of colours and odours: the odour of plants of remote origins mixed with the scent of the tides themselves. The colours create an atmosphere drawn by the objects that reflect them. Light-coloured bright wood and small stones, white marble and adobe, basalt and limestone. The red ash floor contrasts the (more or less) strange plants with long or thick forms having narrow, small, thorny, soft, dark, bright leaves and unknown flowers and fruits. This feeling of oddity and the surprise of a place that suggests another place come about in a spasmodic way along the parallel movement of the ever-present 'sea'. It expands the garden and transforms it into an almost unlimited space like natural spaces. Is it possible for a garden to represent a landscape and mix its limited space with the space of unlimited nature?

Gardens are narrow and long strips of the same width whose length changes as if this dimension depends on what is strictly necessary for this space to become a site. Every garden is a place built on a site. Every garden is a place that configures a landscape. As thought it had created a specific site for each garden, sloping, horizontal or undulating planes form topography. In the depressions, water is collected or is held by slabs. The vegetation stands in such a way that it contains the spaces or directs them. Sometimes it protects them from the sun or wind. Places are built on site: paths mean movements. Landscapes are immense constructions that transform and integrate the underlying nature. Is it possible for a garden to represent a landscape and represent what emerges from need, in that which questions our memory?

Our mind identifies unknown places from those that we know. Our existence in a specific place identifies us with the character of that space and with its substance. Plants and substances shape the garden in different ways: if we build it by repeating the same form with different materials, we will create different places. Perhaps that is where the peculiarity of various places configured by every garden comes from, although we never visited to those remote landscapes. Would it be possible for a garden to represent a landscape through its substance and the spaces that build it?

Then, let us try to walk along unique paths that twist, that stand in parallel, that split and divide themselves, that cross one another until they become mixed up with their order and disorder; the water planes, either still or moving and the sky that contains everything. Perhaps after a while, in the silence that the neighbouring "Sea" gives us, our memory will move towards distinct landscapes that we may not know and that we may never know. Would memory be able to remember what we do not know?

JGDS

Photo Author © Duarte Belo

the afterlife of Garcia de Orta Gardens

Twenty years ago, a sequence of five gardens was created as an homage to *Garcia de Orta* in the context of the 1998 World Expo entitled 'Oceans: a heritage to the future' held in Lisbon. Intended as an open-air pavilion, these gardens represented different places along the ocean coasts from which Garcia de Orta, the famous Portuguese botanist and scientist, collected and studied plants from different continents (India, Asia) and which he presented to Portugal in Europe through his travels over the seas. The scope was scientific in the field of medicine and his book, '*colóquio dos simples e drogues medicines da Índia*' (Goa, 1563), was a descriptive and rich testimony of his research in those distant and unknown places. A plant collection was selected by a group of botanists, landscape-architects and agronomic engineers, sometimes obtaining them from their geographic origins, sometimes from acclimatized origins in Portugal. A landscape architecture design established a linear strip of narrow and long gardens along the River Tejo, creating different atmospheres through spatial and material compositions made of stone, wood, plants, water, soil and concrete, relating to different landscapes in different geographies. The garden acted as a conceptual tool for experience and knowledge as well as a memory device. It was successful during Expo'98 period and its resilient and appreciated design led city authorities not only to preserve it, but to recognize it by awarding a prize (Prémio Valmor 1998). Its strong architectural character survived the growth of the plants, which now dominate the space in scale and material presence. The collection somehow decreased but a significant presence of exotic biodiversity is recognized by assigning the unique presence of certain species. Inhabitants and visitors still search for the garden with its odd experience, sometimes as a kind of thematic space, sometimes through the form of its pavilions among large trees, or the strange combination of unknown plants. It is not a Botanical Garden in the scientific sense but it adds complexity to the botanical experience of Lisbon when visiting other Botanical Gardens like the Garden of the Museum of Natural History (1878), the Royal Botanical Garden of *Ajuda* (1768), or the Tropical Garden at Belém, where a collection of plants from the former Portuguese colonies was installed (1906).

JGDS (2018)

Photo Author © Duarte Belo

Photo Author © Duarte Belo

Photo Author © Duarte Belo

reasoned bibliography

A bibliography on such a specific yet complex theme is not a simple task. In omitting the most technical books of strictly botanical interest and those that are of exceedingly general, the pool of references narrows down. With appropriate exceptions, the botanical garden has rarely been the subject of formal and typological thinking in the recent past. The deterioration of its role as a support for pharmacology has relegated it to a role nearer to that of a garden of pleasure or mass scientific dissemination. A comprehensive scientific dissertation upon the form and typology of the botanical garden is therefore lacking, and so a preliminary step back to a broader context is necessary to find the required links to delineate an initial framework for the topic.

Moreover, the aim of this brief work is, in the end, to merely re-enact, in the public debate, a theme that crosses the disciplines of architecture, landscape and botany (and even archaeology and hydraulics, in the case presented) and hence require a systemic approach : a purpose often sought but seldom practised.

Readers will find some useful starting points for studying the garden (in general) and in particular the botanical garden in a different, more open manner, considering it part of the design domain. This study has benefited from the oeuvre of Monique Mosser and George Teyssot, in particular the Italian edition of "The Architecture of Western Gardens" (Electa, Milano, 1990). This volume, conceived as a set of critical essays on historical issues, supplied the reference framework within which to place the transformations and evolutions that materialised from the "Garden of Botany" over the centuries, helping build those similarities, convergences and divergences that constitute the specificity of the topic. Among these, Lucia Tongiorgi Tomasi's essay, more than others, clarified, hat might be considered the formal archetypes of the modern botanical garden grounded in the middle ages.

Linnaeus' quote *"nomina si nescis perit & cognitio rerum"* is taken from 1751 Edition of *Philosophia botanica*, accessible via OpenLibrary.org, as well as the evocative image of the cabinet. A clarifying account of this heuristic instrument is described in Mueller-Wille S., *Linnaeus' herbarium cabinet: a piece of furniture and its function,* in Endeavour, Volume 30, Issue 2, pp. 60-64 (2006). For insights into the era of the transition from herbaria to computer organization see Shetler S., "The herbarium: past present and future" in Proceedings of the Biological Society of Washington, Vol. 82 pp.687-743 (1969).

An extensive description of the botanical garden is reported in Morton A. G., History of Botanical Science: An Account of the Development of Botany from Ancient Times to the Present Day (Academic Press, Cambridge MA, 1981) and a short but useful account in Spencer R. and Cross R., The origins of botanic gardens and their relation to plant science, with special reference to horticultural botany and cultivated plant taxonomy in Muelleria, Vol. 35, pp. 43-93 (2017). A description of Sennufer's garden can be found in Wilkinson A., *Symbolism and Design in Ancient Egyptian Gardens* in Garden History, Vol. 22, No. 1 (Summer, 1994), pp. 1-17 (1994).

On the relationship between architectural order and knowledge, the rich and extensive work by Martyn Dade-Robertson, The Architecture of information (Routledge, London, 2011), can be considered central. Two works that relate to the topic are Claude Lévi-Strauss' Structural anthropology (Basic Books, New York, 1963) and Michel Foucault's "L'ordine delle cose" (Rizzoli, Milano, 1967). A deep and uncommonly interesting overlook on the relationship between media and architecture is explored in the historical research of Mario Carpo, Architecture in the age of print (MIT Press, Cambridge MA, 2001), and in his The Alphabet and the algorithm (MIT Press, Cambridge MA, 2011).

Enzo Mari's interview is reported in Corriere della Sera, May 1, 2010, of this thinking about agriculture and design can be found both in the exhibition and the essay "Perchè una mostra di falci?/Why an exhibition of sickles?" in OTTAGONO n°100 and in Progetto e passione (Bollati Boringhieri, Milano, 2001). Calvino's quote can be found in "Le città invisibili" (Giulio Einaudi Editore, Turin, 1972), and is also used in the aforementioned works of Martyn Dade-Robertson (2011). Umberto Eco and Jean Claude Carrière, Non sperate di liberarvi dei libri (La nave di teseo, Milan, 2017), makes a point on how new and old media interacts in an apology of the book. Closing the chapter on herbaria are quotes from Jorge Luis Borges, The analytical language of John Wilkins from Other inquisitions (1952) and Umberto Eco, Il nome della rosa (1980)

credits
. . . .

Many people have contributed in various ways to this research and related design work. I must thank them all in these pages because their roles and skills have stimulated my theoretical thinking and practical action.
First and foremost, thanks go to the current director of the Cagliari Botanical Garden, Prof. Gianni Bacchetta, whose vision and hard work created the basic conditions for this project. I would also like to thank the university Chancellor, Prof. Maria Del Zompo, who is always sensitive to the role of the university and its artefacts in the city. Maurizio Usai and Andrea Lallai explained the deep connection between living plant material and garden architecture with great patience. I discussed the relationship between hydraulic engineering and the form of built space with Nanni Sechi and I will continue to do so with pleasure. I constantly discuss the topic of contemporary museography with Paolo Sanjust with whom I often share heterodox positions that lead us down unusual paths. With his uncommon talent, Andrea Forges Davanzati drove our architecture into an unexpected artistic dimension. I would also like to thank Paolo Frau, who in his many roles as Commissioner for Urban Planning and Culture of the City of Cagliari and, above all, as a friend, shared his thoughts and dreams for a renewed city. Joao Gomes Da Silva and Pedro Campos Costa conveyed the extraordinary value of Portuguese architecture and landscape design, stimulating thinking about the making of architecture with elegance and culture. Giaime Meloni's photographs narrate the intrinsic beauty of the banal, the unfinished and the decommissioned. Davide Pisu enriched the content with a decisive contribution that extends its reach to the limits of this text. Barbara Brendolan shared responsibility by radiating competence and trust.
The dedication, inventiveness and devotion of the many young architects who collaborated on this research project have given life to ideas and dreams: Daniela Esu and Giulia Fulghesu (on the underground spaces and entrance pavilion); Nicole Manunza, Valentina Picchiri and Giada Pistis (on the relationship with the Roman Amphitheatre); Mario Callai and Daniela Corona (on the marginal paths and the relationship with the upper city); Nicholas Canargiu, Sara Montis, Andrea Asunis, Federico Melis and Valeria Casciu (on the formal redefinition of the garden). Finally, I want to thank Marcella Aprile whose teachings, balanced between architecture and landscape design, have found renewed meaning in this text.

carnet

carnet

TASSONOMICA
su un orto botanico

Writings of
Giovanni, Marco Chiri; João Gomes da Silva;
Davide Pisu; Giaime Meloni

Author
Giovanni, Marco Chiri

Published by
LISt Lab
info@listlab.eu
listlab.eu

Editorial Director
Alessandro Franceschini

Art Direction & Production
Blacklist Creative Partners, Barcelona
blacklist-creative.com

ISBN 9788899854348

Printed and bound in the European Union,
October 2018

Collection

Prohibited total or partial reproduction of this book by any means, without permission of the author and Publisher.

All rights reserved
© of LISt Lab edition;
© of the author's texts;
© of the author's images;

Promotion and distribution
Messaggerie Libri, Spa, Milano,
Numero verde 800.804.900
assistenza.ordini@meli.it;

International promotion and distribution
ACC Book Distribution Ltd
Woodbridge, Suffolk, IP12 4SD, UK
sales@antique-acc.com

The Scientific Committee of the issues List
Eve Blau (Harvard GSD), Maurizio Carta (University of Palermo), Eva Castro (Architectural Association London) Alberto Clementi (University of Chieti), Alberto Cecchetto (University of Venezia), Stefano De Martino (University of Innsbruck), Corrado Diamantini (University of Trento), Antonio De Rossi (University of Torino), Franco Farinelli (University of Bologna), Carlo Gasparrini (University of Napoli), Manuel Gausa (University of Genova), Giovanni Maciocco (University of Sassari/Alghero), Antonio Paris (University of Roma), Mosè Ricci (University of Trento), Roger Riewe (University of Graz), Pino Scaglione (University of Trento), Claudia Battaino (University di Trento), Luca Zecchin (University di Trento).

LISt Lab is an editorial workshop, based in Europe, that works on contemporary issues. LISt Lab not only publishes, but also researches, proposes, promotes, produces, creates networks.

LISt Lab is a green company committed to respect the environment. Paper, ink, glues and all processings come from short supply chains and aim at limiting pollution. The print run of books and magazines is based on consumption patterns, thus preventing waste of paper and surpluses. LISt Lab aims at the responsibility of the authors and markets, towards the knowledge of a new publishing culture based on resource management.